Red Bird   Ian Roy

BuschekBooks

Ottawa

Library and Archives Canada Cataloguing in Publication

Roy, Ian, 1972-
Red bird / Ian Roy.

Poems.
ISBN 978-1-894543-40-8

I. Title.

PS8585.O89835R44 2007 C811'.6 C2007-901945-5

Credits:
Cover Design by Michael Feuerstack
Photo courtesy of Francine Roy
Photo restoration by Curtis Blondin
Linocut prints by Ian Roy

Printed in Canada by Hignell Book Printing, Winnipeg, Manitoba.

BuschekBooks
P.O. Box 74053
5 Beechwood Avenue
Ottawa, ON K1M 2H9
Canada

BuschekBooks gratefully acknowledges the support of the Canada
Council for the Arts for its publishing program.

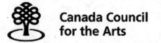

Canada Council   Conseil des Arts
for the Arts   du Canada

for Max and Ari

Table of Contents

Animalia

Some Poems About Photographs

A Letter To Nan Goldin

Traveling, Traveling

Fig. 1

Animalia

Year After Groping Year

The greedy crows watch from the telephone lines
as she digs the small grave.
Soil softly falls from the shovel and slowly covers
the sad, dead body of the dog.
She kneels, pats the soil down and talks
quietly to herself to keep her thoughts from straying
too far out into the field.
(I watch from the porch, suspicious of any words
that might pass between my frozen lips.
Unavailing scarecrow—I cast only shadows.)
She leans her weight on the shovel,
stares down at her hands and asks:
How can I make this year different from the last?

Black Birds

I've been spending a lot of time
staring into the oven lately—
watching pies bake.
It's calming to witness this transition
from not-cooked to cooked;
it makes me think of home,
or, more precisely, *a* home.
And it brings happiness—sometimes
I think it's all I'd like to do with my time:
to bake and bake, until the counter tops
are overflowing with all kinds of pies;
until my family and friends are
stuffed, incapable of even lifting a fork to their mouths;
barely able to nod their heads, thanks.
Only then would I feel complete,
whole, useful, loved.
In the meantime, I'll sit and stare
at the fierce red glowing elements,
and at the baking pies,
turning a deep golden brown.
(As I write this, black birds
eat from the sumac tree outside my window:
poor birds will never taste my pies.)

Packing Plant

The floor in the fish packing plant
glistened with the stringy intestines
of cod and mackerel, of flounder and salmon.
In some places, the worm-ridden insides of the oily fish
lay pulverized in a technicolour paste,
flattened and stretched out
by the thick-soled rubber boots of the plant workers.
Elsewhere, the mess of guts was so thick
that the cement floor could not be seen through the muck.
Here and there were scattered eyeballs,
staring up from the floor,
tails with no heads, heads with no tails,
and myriad scales sparkling on everything in the room
like silver confetti at some gruesome wedding.
And, though it was hard to admit at the time—
in between the nausea and the heaving—
it looked kind of beautiful
in the artificial light:
all those colours, glistening.

Heron

Look, I whispered, pointing to the blue heron
standing motionless in the river.
But I was all alone, and so no one heard me.
The heron remained still, stalking its prey,
or sleeping, or dead from loneliness.
And like the heron, I stood still—
looking down into the river.
Close to the shore, submerged in the water,
rusted out and useless,
was the chassis from an old car. And then,
as my eyes adjusted to the murky green water,
nearly a dozen bicycles came into focus.
And what else? I don't know, deep down in the river.
A thousand other things—lost and forgotten,
stolen and abandoned.
I thought of those things that disappear
when you turn your back,
those *things* that fall into the river,
and rush down stream into the next river,
and the next, and finally out to the open sea
where they are torn apart by the merciless waves
and drowned in the endless black night
that is below the surface of the sea.
When I looked up, the heron had flown off
and in its place, an empty space,
the faint outline of something that had been.

Summer, or When I Was Nine And First Knew Death

From the end of the driveway we watched
as crows circled high above a stand
of birch and maple and spruce.
Turning and turning—
over the trees at the end of the road,
next to a small lake at the bottom of a small hill.
Gulls soon joined in, circling erratically,
diving and carrying on.
The lake was unswimmable because of the weeds
and muck, but it taunted us all the same.
The conspiring trees beckoned like fingers,
motioning for us to come nearer.
But we would have none of it.
Instead, we ran under sprinklers on our unmown lawns,
and then sat eating popsicles,
with the orange or red dye staining our chins.
But we remained aware of the birds circling round.
And of sirens fading in, blaring and fading out.
And the temptation was just too much.
I arrived at the lake in time to see
a man's fully clothed body being pulled onto shore.
Weeds clung to his shoes, to his arms and legs,
and to his hair like a grotesque green wig.
He had a face like melting wax. His mouth
was neither opened nor closed; his eyes, the same.
In an instant, death took on the bloated, pale face
of a murdered man in wet, soiled denim,
replacing the merely ominous cloaked figure
of the grim reaper. Overhead, the birds' angry,
frustrated cries moved beyond the trees,
scattered up the hillside and away.

Birds Hitting Glass

There were nights we would lie awake,
silently watching rain or stars through the window—
or birds hitting glass.
The mornings following those nights
involved silent burials next to the garden,
a shared but separate grief.
Those nights were replaced by darker, longer nights.
You, stumbling down the dark path to our door,
listening carefully for my breath before entering.
And me, pretending to sleep, until sleep found you.
I would open my eyes then, try to make out the shape
of my shoes in the dark, the dim halo of light around the door,
the curve of the handle, the dark path leading away.
We carried on like this until we both got too tired;
and then it was just me, and the birds,
and the closed window.

Fall

I found a live herring—its silvery scales
sparkling in the last afternoon sunlight
under a nearly leafless apple tree.
The fog had only just lifted;
and the sun was not far from setting.
Looking up into the bleached-blue sky,
I guessed that some unlucky gull had dropped the fish
while flying overhead.
This was late fall, you see, and the ground
beneath the tree was covered with dead leaves
and rotten, browning apples.
The herring's slender body—
bluish-green on top, and silver below—
trembled slightly; its tail slapped at some leaves;
a fin worried a worm eaten apple.
One of its murky, grey eyes
stared up into the last remaining leaves of the tree.
Years before this day, when I was eight or nine,
I stood by and watched a boy poke the eyes
from a goldfish with a stick
and then flick them from his finger, laughing;
and I did nothing to stop him.
So—I picked up the herring
and made my way to the beach.
The path was overgrown with tall grass
and weeds. I hadn't noticed
that the herring had stopped moving.
And at the edge of the water, I raised it above my head,
prepared to throw it into the waves—
but I stopped and sighed and stepped
into the frigid Atlantic still wearing my shoes.
The horizon looked as if it had been drawn with a crayon;
I felt like I was stepping into a cartoon.
I'd like to say the herring swam off—gratefully;
that it turned back and waved with one of its little fins.
But it didn't. It floated on the surface of the water,
rising and falling with the waves, slowly being carried out to sea.
I stood and watched until I could no longer feel my feet,
until I could no longer see the herring not-swimming away.

Rats

After the exterminator's visit,
we stopped seeing the rats.
A week passed, and then another:
leaves fell around us like rain.
The gingko leaves dropped all at once:
in a torrent, until the ground
was covered with a faded blanket of yellow.
And like the tree, the sky was also drained of its colour:
there were no changing shades of blue,
no red-sky-at-dawn; but only grey, everywhere,
as if all the colours were sinking deep within the earth,
like so much spilled blood.
The rats were grey and also dirty.
Three weeks after the exterminator's visit,
we found six little corpses
huddled together under some brush:
decomposing, half-eaten by insects,
barely identifiable, except for the tails,
thick and meaty: unchanged.
Snow fell, and the six little graves we dug
vanished into the colourless landscape.

Winter

I am standing alone on a bridge,
suspended between one province and another,
between one city and another one located
somewhere behind me, and
for the first time tonight, I can see the stars.
They are clear and cold in the February sky;
some flicker like distant candle flames,
while others remain constant and true.
I know that some of these stars may well
have burnt out thousands of years ago:
the news just hasn't reached us yet.
Losing the battle between gravity and pressure,
a star will swell like an enlarged heart
before exploding into—sometimes—nothing.
Much closer to earth, the moon appears
as cold and uncertain as the stars.
It casts a shadow of the bridge
down upon the frozen river.
Elsewhere, it illuminates the dirty ice and snow
that has been darkened by falling slush from
passing cars, and the garbage thrown down
by drivers, passengers and pedestrians alike.
The river mirrors the sky in a sort of negative
image: the dark expanse of sky traded
for the whiteness of ice and snow,
the stars exchanged for specks of
garbage and slush.
Down, and to the right, there is
a flashing light—the kind used
to warn drivers of construction on the road.
The light continues to flash,
sending out its warning.
All around it thin crevices like spider webs
have formed during warm spells.
They criss-cross the ice,
adding to the sense of foreboding.
The danger! The hazard! Not far from the light,

there is a bicycle; it was likely stolen
and later abandoned. Someone might
still be looking for it.
The light will eventually stop flashing,
and the ice under it will melt,
sending the doomed amber beacon down
into the dark water below. And the bicycle, too,
will sink, along with all the other debris.
Spring will eventually come and send it all down
river with the fish. But spring still seems far, far away.

The Crying Room

When asked—and it does happen—
I like to tell people I lost my virginity
in the crying room of the W__ movie theatre:
on the floor between the seats,
with someone's chewed gum stuck to my ass
and popcorn crunching beneath us.
If pressed for details, I'll add that
bits of plaster fell like snowflakes
from the ceiling of the dilapidated theatre
and dusted our hair, her back, my shoulders.
I might describe how the light
danced on the walls all around us,
and how the red glow of the exit sign
illuminated her breasts and belly.
I don't mention the crow that was trapped inside the theatre,
or how it flew into the screen
and into the window of the crying room
before falling to the floor exhausted.
I don't mention any of that
because crows flying around inside
bring bad luck, bring death.
But in some tellings I do include the Bergman movie
that was playing in the theatre that night.
And once, I even claimed to hear the squire
utter his final words at the moment of my own sweet triumph:
But feel, to the very end, the triumph of being alive.
But it wasn't really like that at all;
and now the movie theatre is closed,
and for all I know, the seats from the crying room
are on the other side of the country,
in some other movie theatre: or they could be landfill.
And the woman with whom—well, God only knows where she is.
So you see, there is no way I could tell the true story,
because it just can't be done. It can't.

There Is No Path

So, it is almost night,
and the sky is the colour of the fish
I saw floating in the river this morning:
not pink or red, not blue or even grey,
but something like all of those colours
stirred together in a clear plastic bowl.
It gives the sky a warm, menacing beauty;
but with the fish, it reminded me of bile—
or at least the word *bile*.
And now, looking up at this sky is a little
like looking up at the pale undersides of the dead fish
from somewhere far below,
from within the muck and the weeds
at the bottom of the river. It feels a little like that, too.
And with the sun slowly being removed from the equation,
the light is haunting, ominous.
That's when I see it flying over the city,
with a quiet that is breathtaking:
a great blue heron. And I'm certain—
certain! that it is the same one I saw last year:
on the rock, and in the river, and over the river.
That very one. So quiet,
until nothing else matters—
none of these *feelings*, none of these *problems*.
It's just me and the heron: and everything else freezes.
The traffic stops, the lights stop changing, the clouds—
they stop floating across the sky so carelessly;
not one breath is exhaled,
not one drop of spit hits the sidewalk.
Aw, come on, try to imagine it:
there is nothing, there is no path.
It's just you and the heron—silent wings,
swimming through the air. It doesn't even notice
you down there. But you watch it,
and feel a part of its movement:
somehow, in some dislocated, fantastic way,

you feel a part it—
And then it's gone. And it's only you, the clouds
once again gliding past, the lights changing from red
to green, and the darkness descending like a curtain on a stage.

The Moth

There's a dead moth on my desk,
and it's been here for months.
Small dusty wings, flecked brown and grey;
miniscule antennae, bent and useless;
and the furry sliver of a body:
all together, no bigger than my thumbnail.
And when I sigh, which I do often these days,
the air leaves my mouth, drifts
invisibly across my desk,
and little wings tremble nervously.
But then they settle, I settle, we settle
back into this dark space of waiting
that is nowhere, nothing.

Another Poem About Birds

The bird fluttered weakly
beneath the weight of the wet towel
my neighbour had thrown over it.
I watched as he pulled the bird out
and broke its neck with one quick,
fatal movement of his fleshy hands.
It was done in a way
that suggested practice, or at least *experience.*
He gave it a shake; looked on approvingly
as the bird's head flopped from side to side:
limp, rubbery, lifeless.
My neighbour eats pigeon, I whispered.
Or is that *pigeons?* But that
is not what this is about anymore
than it's about the emptiness of the sky
when all the birds have gone south. Or,
my heart. Later, I watched as he sat
and plucked feathers from the dead bird,
and I watched as a small gust of wind
picked up some of those feathers and carried them away.
They flew up and up,
and floated down and down,
and were then lost from sight, from my sight.
Back on the balcony, the door was closing
behind my neighbour and the bird
and also, I imagined, a pot of boiling water on the stove,
a knife and fork laid out on the table—
my heart, my heart.

Feathers Fly, Seasons Change

This old house is made of moss and dirt,
lead-based paint and rotting lumber—
breathing is difficult here.
A bird hit the kitchen window this afternoon.
I heard the thud from the next room—
a dizzy spell had laid me down on the floor—
and when I looked up and out the window
all I saw was the clear summer day,
the green leaves of the apple tree waving gently
and a single cloud that looked—
if I were pressed to come up with a comparison—like a moose
rearing on its hind legs.
At night: it's all stars and darkness here,
fireflies and the gentle, sleepy lowing of cows in the distance.
Picture perfect, on the outside.
Inside, it is another story;
inside it is always storming.
I had to stand up to see it,
crumpled on the driveway beneath the window:
a small sparrow lay dead.
And that damn feral cat already approaching, stage left.
I knocked on the window but the cat ignored me.
She pissed on the porch
when I refused her entry the day I moved in:
just squatted and pissed and then walked away.
So that's the kind of cat she is.
I stepped outside, nauseous and weak,
and struggled with a shovel for ten minutes.
No more ceremonies, just piles of dirt and *meaningful* silences.
Well, the dead birds are piling up in this book:
a small mountain of hollow-boned, winged-death.
Even in the sun, even in the rain,
feathers fly, seasons change:
I am breaking under the weight of these
poor dumb creatures. I don't know
how much more I can take. And that cat
is already scratching at the grave. Guess I'll
be digging a new one in the morning.

Fauna

Okay, so now I have felt death with my own hands—
the limp bloodlessness of it, the weakness of it.
And I've had its smell linger on my clothes
so that people have asked:
Where have you been?
My fear is that you will never forgive me.
It was me, after all, who held you down on the metal table
while the vet pushed the needle into your leg.
You hissed and scratched at me—
and I saw that look you gave me.
But within seconds, like air leaving a balloon: nothing.
Nothing but fur and bones, your eyes closed.
And I know, I know you could care less;
this is about me, right?
But when I felt you go limp, and
when I could no longer hold back,
and just cried and cried and had to leave, crying,
I thought that maybe I had finally learned something
about life, and about death.
And about all these mistakes I keep making:
but in the end, I know, what I've learned
could not fill your empty bowl,
could not even fill a whisper in your dead and dying ear.

Some Poems About Photographs

Preface, or There is the paper and then there is the person

I went to the archives to get an accurate
account of the weather for that day:
January 19, 1981—
This will be the only thing that I can say
with any certainty. So, we'll start there,
with the weather, and it will be
like small small-talk—the sun shone brightly,
but it was cold; the temperature hovered
somewhere below zero, so that from above
pedestrians looked like little steam-engines
puffing up and down the sidewalks—
their breath appearing and then disappearing
right before their eyes.
Then we'll move on to a photograph:
another self-portrait, sent as a postcard.
There is a knife held in her hand like an
upside down pendulum keeping time with her heart;
and something—is it blood?—oozing from her breast,
around a strip of photo-booth portraits
that appear cut free from her chest.
Our eyes move involuntarily back to the knife,
and notice—with relief—that it does not drip blood.
Turn the picture over to reveal her handwriting
on the back: a series of uneven lines, illegible
at times but telling in their own way.
She once held a pen like a knife,
ink flowed like blood from a wound.
The rest is conjecture or anecdote:
a story left behind like a strand of hair
trapped between the pages of a favourite book—
arrogant in its outlasting; or like the memories
that follow us wherever we go—
confused with photography; fused with our history.
(Let this be our introduction.)

Dragonfly

She'd been told that a dragonfly
would come and sew her lips shut if she told a lie

—and so she tries hard not to lie:
especially outdoors, in the summer.

As she runs around the yard,
the dragonflies lift and fly in unison

like small helicopters hovering over the grass;
they scan the yard for somewhere safe to land

and resume whatever it is they do all day.
Under the brilliant New Hampshire sun,

she watches, astounded, as two of them
couple in flight: their translucent wings—

veined and shimmering—
flutter and beat against one another.

It appears to occur as if by accident;
like they just flew into one another and—oops.

A dragonfly alights on her shoulder
and she thinks, quickly: have I told any lies today?

Swan Song (Providence)

The contrast of the surrounding darkness
serves to focus the eyes:
we are not meant to avert our gaze.
Pale skin, and head turned slightly
away, she lays upon a white table or bench,
or perhaps just a cold slab of wood.
Legs hang off the side,
feet lost in dark space;
she holds on with thin arms,
hands hidden beneath, fingers gripping.
There is an obvious reference
to the crucifixion at work here:
though what you make of it,
remains up to you.
It is from a handbill announcing
an early show in Providence.
She is nude; and at her pubis is a stuffed,
long billed bird, another bird rests between her breasts:
their wings extend outward, as if in flight.
She named it swan song;
the photo is taken from bird's-eye-view.
It seems too quiet to be meant to shock;
the lines are graceful, the birds are peaceful
(though of course, they are dead).
Did I mention that her eyes are closed?

Door

The first thing you see is a door, seemingly suspended
as if by some illusion—but delicately balanced
against a wall at an awkward angle, teetering.

The scene is lit from an open window
but the light stops at the door, slicing
the room in two, leaving shadows, dark corners.

To the right, a vacant doorway, leading to another room,
more doorways. A pipe runs up the wall beside the first door:
plumbing, an afterthought maybe forty years later

in this building in Providence. The long hardwood
planks of the floor are rough, wax-less,
strewn with plaster from the falling-down walls.

The room is an array of lines and angles, light and shadow.
And of course, beyond the camera's view,
somewhere behind—right where you are looking from, in fact—

stood the photographer. After arranging the door against the wall,
after waiting for the ideal light: the shutter snapped.
There is no way of knowing what happened next.

House

I

In that broken down room in Providence,
the sun burned holes through the walls;
it caused the plaster to crumble and fall,
it peeled the wallpaper and dropped it to the floor.
Outside the window, the outline
of trees, haloed and glowing,
but removed and indistinct.

II

In my broken down house,
the one I lived next to as a kid,
all I ever thought to do was snoop around
at the things left behind by the former tenants.
Boxes of…what? Loose papers and greeting cards.
Wooden spoons and broken picture frames. Old plates,
and cracked tea cups. Cutlery. *Why so much cutlery?*
And moldy books, some of which I brought home
and read: inhaling spores and words simultaneously.
And that box of photographs.

III

Beneath the window,
partly obscured by a sheet
of cracked and faded wallpaper,
is the blurred shadow of a face, soon to be absent.
One foot pushes into the foreground:
a pale leg catches the light,
and a buckled shoe steps into the debris.

IV

I kept some of the photographs I found—
between the pages of a favourite book, where they remain today.
But the house is gone: trees grow in its place.
And I no longer live next to what is now a wooded lot.
The photos show a family at the beach, or the same family
on Christmas morning.
In all of them, they are smiling, all of them.
They are strangers to me, these people.

V

The walls became me, I gave in to the room
and was transformed: it is like living in the same house
for too long. The smell becomes a part of you—
like a leech—it remains with you,
no matter how many bodies of water
you cross. It becomes a place you wear
in your eyes, in your hair, in the way you leave a room.

VI

There was another house—much later,
and since abandoned by me—where
in the morning, before coffee,
I swept flakes of dried ceiling paint
from the kitchen floor; later, I picked it out of my cereal bowl,
my hair. I have kept that room with me,
and all the rooms, like a paint chip that fell into my pocket,
and remains there, always.

A Train Leaving the Station

This is what she saw from the train: the dirty secrets
of small towns—the things one sees when entering
unannounced from the backdoor: the dirty dishes

in the sink, dust balls the size of soccer balls in the dark
corners of the room, the crumbs on the floor,
the dried up strand of spaghetti stuck to the wall

above the stove. She saw cemeteries with fresh mounds of
dark, overturned soil; cannibalized cars in the backyards
of small homes; the unpainted backsides of buildings;

the stinking garbage dump, with its diving gulls, muted through
the window; a family standing by the side of the tracks,
sad-eyed and perhaps lost—

No, no, wait. That was what I saw from the train.
And I tried to imagine that she saw these same things,
which she may have—but it's not likely.

All that she saw, she may have seen through the lens
of her camera; she may have slept through the entire journey.
And that family, they wouldn't have been there.

(I wonder sometimes if I really saw them; and what, exactly,
did they see?—the lights of the train? the windows?
me staring down at them?) I'll never really know for sure.

San Lorenzo

She was in half light—half shadow;
sometimes there was only darkness.

She smuggled angel-wings, bags of live eels—her props—
past the first floor guard, and up to the abandoned spaghetti factory
in San Lorenzo. (She joked that Americans thought spaghetti
grew on trees, not letting on that she was American.)

At night, with a frayed rope tied to a basket,
she'd haul up *cornetti* and *cappucino* from the second floor window
of her studio—waving to the people below, careful not to spill.
Her camera hung from her shoulder.
One day melted into the next—on film,

the failing light of each day shifted in hazy tones.
At night, there were candles for light, or the streetlights outside,
or, the moon. On her last night, she watched from the window
as a man walked his bicycle past. She was drawn
to his song of unrequited love. His voice

was as straight as the *via dei Coronari*. He sang
and walked down the center of the first straight road in Rome;
and she was his only audience.
The next morning she kissed the ground—

and with gravel stuck to her moist lips,
she boarded her flight for home.

Postcard from New York

This city takes its toll. I want Rome—
but it's not the city, I realize, not the lights,
not the buildings forcing long shadows—
the windows at the top reflecting the light of the sun
but not its warmth, not the people in cars,
not the smog filled streets that choke me
mornings, not the cabs—yellow streaks across the city—
just a hand reaching across a table to rest on mine—
briefly—or to brush the hair from my face; the wink
of an eye; or a smile. The smallest gesture could save me,
keep me here forever.

Rome

The silence of the scene is what strikes you—

an empty chair in the foreground,
the quiet of held breath in the background,

an averted face. Her flesh looks like paper:
pale and thin, nearly translucent.

She hangs by her finger tips from the door frame.
Her toes point to the floor like small, blunt arrows.

Light enters from the right—an early morning light?
In the photo, she still somehow breathes, is alive
(a trick with the camera).

She becomes weightless and then winged—
blurred before your eyes,

she rises to the top of the frame, up and out.

Ravenna

The church was bombed during the last war;
a *trompe l'oeil* covers the upper half of the wall:
a tomb. (Somewhere, in another room,
tourists follow a guide who explains
the cement restoration of the bottom half
of the wall, the burial rituals, the Italian names
of columns, of painting techniques. She left the group behind,
to find this room, use it for a backdrop in another
portrait.) And she is a blurred combination of light and dark—
indistinct, perhaps smiling, perhaps not—as clothes fall
before the tomb; her legs and torso meld into the gray
(restored) wall as she shifts and moves, hurrying to get the shot.
Lines on the marble floor lead directly to her; the shutter again,
and then clothes pulled on quickly before the tourists
turn the corner into this room.

Here Comes The Light

You open the door and see her, almost naked, shivering—
waiting for the perfect slant of light to enter
the room, transform it into something ethereal and
mysterious. To her left, plucked white angel-wings hang

eerily suspended from the ceiling. A long, thin wire extends
from the camera across the room to her small, pale hand—
trembling with the cold. You realize the sound you heard
was her teeth chattering, and that is what led you up there:

that almost imperceptible sound. She waves at you,
oblivious to the cold, to her goose-pimpled skin:
I'm just waiting, she says. *Any moment now...*
And it does happen: suddenly, the light is staggering,

illuminating the wings from behind; long, thin shadows
are cast across the floor to the opposite wall.
She moves and is a blur; she waves you away.
And leaving, all you hear is the chattering of the shutter

clicking like morse code.

The Eel

Beginning in darkness and slipping into light
like a photograph developed in reverse.
All around her, the eels. Imagine the bucket
that carried them to her studio: full and alive,
moist eyes staring up menacingly at nothing;
and then dead and slick: a bucket full of darkness.
Did she buy them at the local market? Or maybe
from some kids at the shore? Would she have told
them what she had planned for the eels? That
they were props to be photographed:
delicately arranged around sliced lemons on a table,
in a bowl, on the floor? Or did she simply smile,
and say nothing? In the photograph,
she has an inscrutable look on her face.
And while she is naked, and on her knees—
holding one of the eels close to her body,
letting it curve around her breast like some shadowy,
second skin—it is not erotic, exactly.
There is in it her determined concentration,
and maybe wonderment at her mysterious experiment,
all those lines and curves emerging from light,
and ending in shadow.

New Hampshire

We imagine a change in her eyes,
in the way she looks at the camera;
we can see it; we're all so sure of this.

(We're also stubborn and naïve.)
Her arms are covered in birch bark.
It isn't hard to imagine roots growing

from the soles of her feet,
buried somewhere beneath,
in the cold, hard New Hampshire soil,

wrapped around stone and earth,
slithering past the roots of other trees.
And her arms stretching up and out,

and leaves sprouting from the tips of her fingers,
pulling in the light,
and turning it into darkness.

Red Bird

She was last seen alive—wearing a loose red summer dress,
a camera bag hanging from one bare shoulder
—walking into an abandoned building on 7th Avenue.

Missing stairs like a child's mouth: empty spaces
where teeth should be, or had been.
Ornate cracks spider-webbing across the walls.
Wallpaper stretching down to the floor:
peeling away from the memory of glue.

It astounded her to find this here, in the midst
of this sometimes filthy city, something so beautiful.

It becomes a dream or a movie: anything but real.
Soft, sparse music begins as she breaks through glass.
She falls in slow motion to a waltz. And when she lands,
it is not on the roof of a cab, not in front of horrified pedestrians,
but on a forgiving, air-filled mattress. She rises—
amazed at the stunt—brushes herself off and squints up
into the sunlight as she traces with her finger

an invisible line from the window to where she now stands.

A Letter To Nan Goldin

A Letter To Nan Goldin

Dear Nan, I'm so tired.
And here I am—I know this is no way to start a letter but—
here I am after a good night's sleep,
seated at a maple desk, next to a wall of glass
in the most beautiful library in town
(and I know libraries, Nan, I do: I do).
And outside these windows, across a verdant hilly field,
just beyond a statue of Champlain
with his upside-down astrolabe,
is a bridge I have walked across so many times,
a bridge which spans a river
I have spent many hours watching.
The sky is endless blue today, reflected in the river.
Boats pass by below, and the passengers smile and wave
to the people on the shore.
And I love all of these things, Nan:
I love to *bear witness* to this life
that resides so close by, but out of reach.
And, oh, I have a family, too, Nan:
I am so lucky to have a beautiful, loving family
to wake up to every morning—and between clean sheets.
I awake between clean, crisp white sheets.
(This is important to me, Nan. It is.
And I only mention it because sitting here,
looking at these photographs of
you and your friends, I feel—
please don't take this the wrong way but—dirty.)
And I'm exhausted, suddenly, and feeling
terribly down and broken-hearted.
I'm broken-hearted, Nan, torn in two.
And I'm looking at a photograph of you.
You know the one, the self-portrait with the black eyes.
And I feel, all of a sudden, as if I've swallowed my own heart—
Or, as if my heart is, *all of a sudden*, in my stomach.
And it beats down there, out of place, out of whack:
a heart in two unevenly beating pieces,
hiding somewhere behind my navel,

in the boiler-room of my guts, scared and worried.
It's a strange feeling, Nan.
I'm not trying to be poetic here:
I really think it's there, I do.
You'd be able to see it on an x-ray.
But right now, Nan, all I want is
to have you reassure me that...what?
That everything is going to be okay? Maybe you'd only laugh,
and punch me in the arm. So, I'll change the page.
And your friend is dying right there, on the page.
And another: oh, it hurts just to look. There's you
on the train, after rehab. But the colours,
I know, the colours are beautiful, they are:
and so rich, and more real than real. And in some
photos your friends smile or laugh or fuck;
and they're in love with you: all of them.
And it's good to have friends to love,
and to have those that love you right back:
I know this, Nan. I do. Because I have friends
and I love them all.
Nan, I want more than anything to know
that you are happy now.
And then I'll change this page, too.
I am the young man who fainted after that slide show
in Paris. And I am the one who couldn't walk by
but did walk by in Chicago.
It hurts to know so much about you, Nan.
To know so much, and to not know anything
at all. To know these two things simultaneously: well,
it hurts my head.
Okay, Nan, I'm done. And maybe I'm a little drunk
right now. And maybe I'm not where I say I am
but someplace else I don't love so much;
and all of my dear friends and family, Nan,
maybe they are not here with me,
but someplace else I don't love so much.
But I'll still feel this way when the sun comes up.
I'll awake with your landscapes in my head:
my eyes swimming in the azure seas.
Everything will be still then, Nan,

and I will stand up and walk into the river
and swim out into the open water beneath the bridge:
and I'll wave to that young man in the library
seated at the maple desk next to the window,
looking at photographs of you and your friends: at all of you.
And I will wave, and he might mistake it for
me drowning, asking, begging for help. But
there will be nothing he can do.
Nothing at all. So he'll just turn away,
and pretend he doesn't see me.
And then maybe I will drown in all of this;
or I will sink beneath the sky-blue surface of the river
and grow fins and gills and silvery scales,
and swim off to some other place, so far from here.
I've included a self-addressed stamped envelope
so that you might write me back sometime.
I hope you do, Nan. I really hope you do.
     Yours, etc.
        I. Roy

Traveling, Traveling

When I Think of Leaving

I think of you, and that August night so long ago.
The weather had already turned;
and after a couple months of sunlight,
night was on its way just as I was on my way.
Up above, in this newly black sky,
I saw the northern lights for the first time:
not fireworks at all, as I had hoped,
but waves of colour, red and green,
as if blowing in the wind,
rippling and snapping like a sheet on a line, or like a flag,
but with the sound turned off.
I vowed to return the following year:
after school and loose-ends—were not loose anymore.
And the next day, driving south,
I nearly turned back several times:
ready to give up my other life back home,
and remain there with you
to watch winter burst forth in all its supposed harshness.
To hole up someplace and watch it from a window.
But I kept driving, even when
those pheasants appeared on the road before me;
unable to brake in time, I kept driving:
in a blast of feathers and birds.
I could not turn back, not anymore.
And then years passed,
and still I have not been back.
But I think of it every August:
all those birds—I don't know how many—and
the blood and feathers stuck to the grill,
and one in-tact wing hooked on
to the bumper.
I see it when I close my eyes,
and then it's gone.

While Two Mute Friends Slept Nearby Dreaming of Flight

Crossing over from the Island,
I watched as the full moon rose out of the Strait
like a helium balloon:
and I thought I knew happiness.
But then I wound up on that picnic table,
as if waiting for the surgeon to arrive.
In my sleeping bag, staring up at the stars overhead,
I counted—no, not sheep—kilometres on my fingers
and toes, and then used the stars themselves:
counting ever higher, but never reaching that elusive number
that would guarantee sleep. Instead, I imagined ways
of securing myself to the table so that I would not fall off
in the night; but I had no rope, not even a single shoelace—
and it was just as well. I worried about concussions
and wet grass. Highway traffic hummed
in the distance throughout the night
so that it sounded—after awhile—like wind through trees
or water falling. And that would have been *OK, just fine.*
But by morning, the noise grew worse,
and it was impossible to pretend that it was anything
but traffic.

Alberta

Like giant candles on a birthday cake,
towers tipped with flames rose above the trees.
This was in Northern Alberta, at dusk.
At the time, they were mysterious and new,
and also ominous—
I thought of you asleep beside me,
and how you would not always be there.
I would see them only that once,
and then never again.

Saskatchewan

Parked beneath a pale weeping willow—
sick from exhaust, the dead and dying branches
sweeping across the ground—
I awoke to the sound of a crop duster flying overhead,
and thought of that scene in *North By Northwest*.
The plane roared past and began spraying the vast fields of canola
just beyond—like some golden sea that stretched toward the horizon.
Years later, I would watch that Hitchcock movie again
in an apartment in Halifax, and the following afternoon
my first son would be born. It is like this, we begin.

When It Began

Your cheeks burned red and our hands touched accidentally; or,
our hands touched accidentally and your cheeks burned red.
And when the door opened, and a shadow fell across the room—
literally fell across the room—it crushed us both beneath it.
And then we two were silent slips of shadows,
and everything was changed, and always would be so.

Quebec

Unfailingly, but with great *failure!*
something always goes wrong.
Between here and there. And somewhere
in between all of this: a flat tire, a broken
hose, a hole in the exhaust.
Or, worse, things we can't name
or say aloud: a whispered illness in the backseat,
a word that makes you giggle nervously
the way children do sometimes
at something they don't—or can't—understand.
Something always goes wrong;
and we stopped watching
French films because of it.
The word *harbinger* comes to mind.
Good night, good night:
sang the barber to his lover,
sang the butcher to the lamb.
(When the lights of the city came into view—
or were they receding?—I swerved into the ditch,
and waited for morning light,
because I always make better choices
in the morning.)

**Of Places I Have Slept And Later Regretted: Exhibit A, or
I Sat and Watched It Fall Apart, But I Was No Accomplice**

In Moncton, New Brunswick, the nights
are long and you think mostly of
leaving, but also—and sadly—
of staying. The nights are long and
seem not to end; you think in terms
of what was, or what could have been:
it is all so clear when you leave
that city, but at the time, well,
it is not so clear. At night, you
watch the trains leave, and the buses
with sleepy passengers aching
for cigarettes, their foreheads pressed
against the windows so that their
faces no longer look like their
faces. And in the morning when
you awake, the city is still
dark. In Moncton, New Brunswick, the
light falls through every crack in the
pavement, the river dries up, things
start to crumble. And you hear the
thunder, and you see the lightning,
but no rain, not a drop of rain.

Of Places I Have Slept And Later Regretted: Exhibit B, or And Then It Happened To Me, Though I Thought It Never Could

In Mexico, Maine, the nights are
long, you think mostly of leaving,
of where you came from and where you
are going. You think of yellow
lines, curved roads, headlights reflected
in the eyes of deer, and all of
those missed opportunities: the
ones behind, and the ones yet to
come. In the morning, the ground is
damp and trampled, slugs cling to blades
of grass, the birds' cries sound harsh and
cracked, so unlike the ones *back home*.
But the same dark clouds hang heavy
overhead, the same dark feeling
in your gut. In Mexico, Maine,
there are no sandy beaches, no
cool waters to break through, to wake
you in the morning; no breakfast
diners with laughing waitresses
and surly but smiling cooks. You
drive until you find such things, you
don't stop until you find these things.

Of Places I Have Slept And Later Regretted: Exhibit C, or The Highway Was Flooded, How Would We Ever Get Home?

In Burlington, Vermont, the nights
are long and you think mostly of
leaving, but only to return
the following day with a mid-
size trailer carrying all your
possessions—even the knick-knacks
you always try to give away
to friends: even the books you still
haven't read and maybe never
will. In the morning, with the sun
reflecting off Lake Champlain, you
listen to the weather report,
you scan the horizon for storm
clouds: and there they are, to the north,
they are always there; and the washed
out highways of Montreal. And
sure, you can head west, but for how
long? In Burlington, Vermont, you
put another quarter into
the parking meter, stall just a
little longer. Because what else
is there for you to do? *What else?*

Ohio

Off the highway outside of Sandusky,
under the raucous glow and subsequent
haze of Independence Day fireworks,
I fell asleep on the passenger side.
As the fireworks ended, a heavy and pungent
smoke drifted and descended, filling my dreams
with gunpowder. Earlier in the night,
driving west on the I-90,
I had to turn off the tape deck. Tom Waits
making the dark, lonely Ohio night,
an even darker, lonelier night.
And of course, Neil Young was also out of
the question. And so, it was forward. And AM radio
playing—of course—The Eagles;
and when I started singing along,
I knew that it was time to pull-over.
In the morning, I woke to gunfire or to fireworks
or to the memory of both still ringing in my ears.
And for a moment—for one brief, sweet moment,
I had no idea where I was.
I drove all that day,
out of Ohio as if shot from a cannon,
straight through to Iowa, and on and on.
Weeks would pass before I could turn around
and go home. And many more after that,
before I could listen to Tom Waits, or
even think of looking at a map.

Iowa

We stood at the center of that night in Iowa,
slowly spinning round to take it all in:
it was hard to tell where the fireflies ended
and where the stars began.
So much darkness, and so far from home.
We convinced ourselves that the forest
was full of one-eyed black cats,
their luminous eyes repeatedly blinking
through the darkness among the trees,
and their long, skinny tails waving.
like the tall grass we couldn't see.

Colorado

I learned fear in Colorado,
but also love.
Driving over a mountain pass during a rainstorm,
with a hundred—no, a two-hundred foot drop to my right:
a long way down and only a tin-foil railing
between me and all of that nothing.
A narrow two-lane, the oncoming cars,
and the back and forth of the useless wipers.
I remembered that as a child I hid
my face every time we crossed a bridge:
and later, the nightmares about bridges,
and, of course, falling.
Driving in the car that day in Colorado,
no one spoke, no one said anything.
I turned off the radio. And I tried not to—
but I did imagine careening off the cliff,
and falling into I know not what:
the impossible grey fog—
or were they clouds so heavy,
they had sunk from the sky to surround us?
And me falling, falling all that way down.
I thought of how I would miss you,
and how I hoped you would miss me, too.

Utah

I run my hand over the map, concentrating on the contours
that are there, or not there: the borders, the warmth of highway
asphalt, the cool wetness of the great salt lake, the dryness
of the glimmering salt flats. The names of towns
I think I could fall in love with.
My fingers come to rest on a town just east of here—where
I know I could find you if I just opened my eyes—I fold the map,
taking note of every crease and tear—and head west through
a state that terrifies me with its test sites and gambling,
with its long stretches of highway going nowhere, fast.
I've got nowhere to be, but I'm in a hurry.
The lights of all-night gas stations provide the best light
for taking pictures of friends—that aren't here with me, now.
Creased and cracked. I noticed wrinkles
in the corners of my eyes this morning—if I open them
wide enough, they disappear; if I close them tight
enough—closed, it all disappears.

Nevada

For many miles there really was nothing
but highway, desert, and long fences that warned:
KEEP OUT! HIGH SECURITY AREA.
Oh, and the small towns boasting these three things:
gas station, convenience store, and casino.
But then this: a long switchback twisting its way up
the side of Angel Mountain at impossible angles.
And further up—remarkably—snow in July
and the slow steady trickle down
into the mouth of the cool, cool Angel Lake.
Where the road ended, a family was parked
on a green battered sofa, as though perched
on a giant mound of lichen. Their pick-up sat nearby,
radio playing hits of yesterday and today.
From behind: three fishing rods pointed to the blue sky,
lines falling down into the water, disappearing
into the smooth black surface of Angel Lake.
Jesus walking on the water would not
have disturbed their determined concentration.
A boy and his parents. In my mind, he forever
has a potato chip held half-way between the bag
and his mouth; and from the mouths of his parents,
cigarettes dangle, forgotten, ashes hanging limp
like arthritic index fingers, resigned to forever point downward.
Beside the sofa, a bucket of fish:
each one still squirming, thinking maybe it's still not too late.
And the sun setting somewhere behind them,
devouring their shadows, ending the day,
night falling down upon us all like a big, black net.

Oregon

We ditched the car, and hitch-hiked south through Oregon
—heading for California and its dirty beaches and sand castles
(its broken dreams). We spent a night outside a small town
with the same name as my grandmother—I wanted to find
some memento to send her, proof—but by morning we were gone.
That night, though, in Oregon, I slipped out after dark,
quietly—not wanting to wake my fellow travelers. The sky
like the roof of my tent, the stars like the holes that let in
rain. I ran for the highway: aiming, I thought, north: home.
I walked in the ditch, on the shoulder: the lights of
passing cars illuminated me, freezing me against
the backdrop of trees—the lights of the 400 angels
of death left me motionless by the side of highway 101.
It wasn't long before I saw a sign telling me I was again heading
south—away—I fell to the grass and let the lights pass over me—
and then I was back in my tent.
In the morning I took a photograph of my hand
against the backdrop of the rising sun—the only proof I have
that I was ever in Oregon.

California

I think of the two of you
driving through a garden of wind turbines
in the Silicon Valley,
the others asleep in the back of the van.
Hundreds of thin white windmills like giant
long-necked cranes in the half-light of that morning;
silent mirages to the sleepers.
The pale light of the dashboard,
the cool windshield
when you reach forward to touch,
an empty highway.
There is a photograph: grainy and tentative;
the sun, not yet risen, but glowing faintly
on the horizon.
If you stare unblinking,
the long, white blades break loose
and fly up into that cloudless sky,
wings suddenly, flapping,
growing smaller and smaller
and then disappearing;
all of it,
disappearing.

Washington

Even our footsteps in the wet sand
illuminated the phosphorescence,
green flickering light following behind
and then disappearing like a trail of bread crumbs
eaten by black birds in a fairy tale.
And then those boys, rowing in from who-knows-where,
their paddles disturbing the dinoflagellates
in the water, the light erupting like fireworks.
It was night, the moon high and small in the starry sky.
The boys pulled their boat up onto the sand,
and then silently lit cigarettes.
They nodded hello as we passed by,
and then went back to staring out at the sea.
Walking away and looking back at them,
the ends of their lit cigarettes looked like
more phosphorescence, orange creeping light,
repeating a slow dance, up and then down,
and then up again, before finally falling to the ground,
and being extinguished underfoot;
the green light extending outwards like lightning.

Lullaby

She sings a slow sad song; and like a whisper in my ear,
it floats in from the next room. The house is quiet;
the boys will soon be asleep. Snow continues to fall,
small flakes that blow this way and that.
Everything outside is buried under snow and has been
for too long now. Cars drive past, and I imagine the wet sound
of tires rolling through the snow,
the hissing of snowflakes as they land and melt
on the warmed hoods of the cars.
My work is going slowly, but going—I tell
anyone who asks. The song makes its way to me once again;
her voice, softer now, like a hummingbird's fluttering wings.
City noises filter in persistently: the cars and trucks,
the murmuring of people on their way through the streets,
the city. *We all have places to be*, the song ends,
we all have places to be.
Someone is coming, and someone is going.
And tomorrow is another day.

Acknowledgements

Some of these poems first appeared in: *The Antigonish Review, Arc, Descant* and *Grain.* The author would like to extend his thanks to the editors, past and present, of those fine journals. He would also like to gratefully acknowledge the Ontario Arts Council and the City of Ottawa for financial support in the form of arts grants during the writing of this book. And of course, many thanks go out to family and friends.

Notes

"Year after Groping Year" borrows its title from a line in the book *Pilgrim at Tinker Creek* by Annie Dillard.

"Some Poems About Photographs": The poems in this section were inspired by the work and life of the photographer Francesca Woodman (1958-1981).

"Preface, or There is the paper and then there is the person" borrows the second half of its title from a line in the book *On Photography* by Susan Sontag.

"A Letter To Nan Goldin": Nan Goldin is a photographer whose work is stunningly personal, and personally stunning.

About the Author

Ian Roy's previous book, *People Leaving,* was short-listed for both the Upper Canada Writers' Craft Award and the City of Ottawa Book Award. His work has appeared in numerous magazines, including *Arc, Descant* and *Geist.* His short-story, "Family", was recently included in the anthology, *Decalogue 2.* He lives in Ottawa.